**All rights are reserved.**
No part of this publication may be reproduced, stored in a retrieval system or
transmitted in any form or by any means, electronic,
mechanical, photocopying, recording or otherwise, without
written permission of the publisher. For more information regarding permission, email to

TheDimplePuppet@icloud.com

TheDimplePuppet Publishing

First Edition

Copyright © 2016 Andre L. Simmons

All rights reserved.

ISBN-13: 978-0692741863 (Custom Universal)

ISBN-10: 0692741860

**Printed in the U.S.A.**

# Little Kinky Kiki

By: Andre L. Simmons

# Kiki

# Shrinkage

Kiki's father just shampooed his daughter's hair; she looked up at him as he finished patting it dry.

"Daddy?" Ask Kiki.

"Yes?" He responded.

"I don't like getting my hair conditioned and shampooed." Said Kiki.

"Why is that?" He asked.

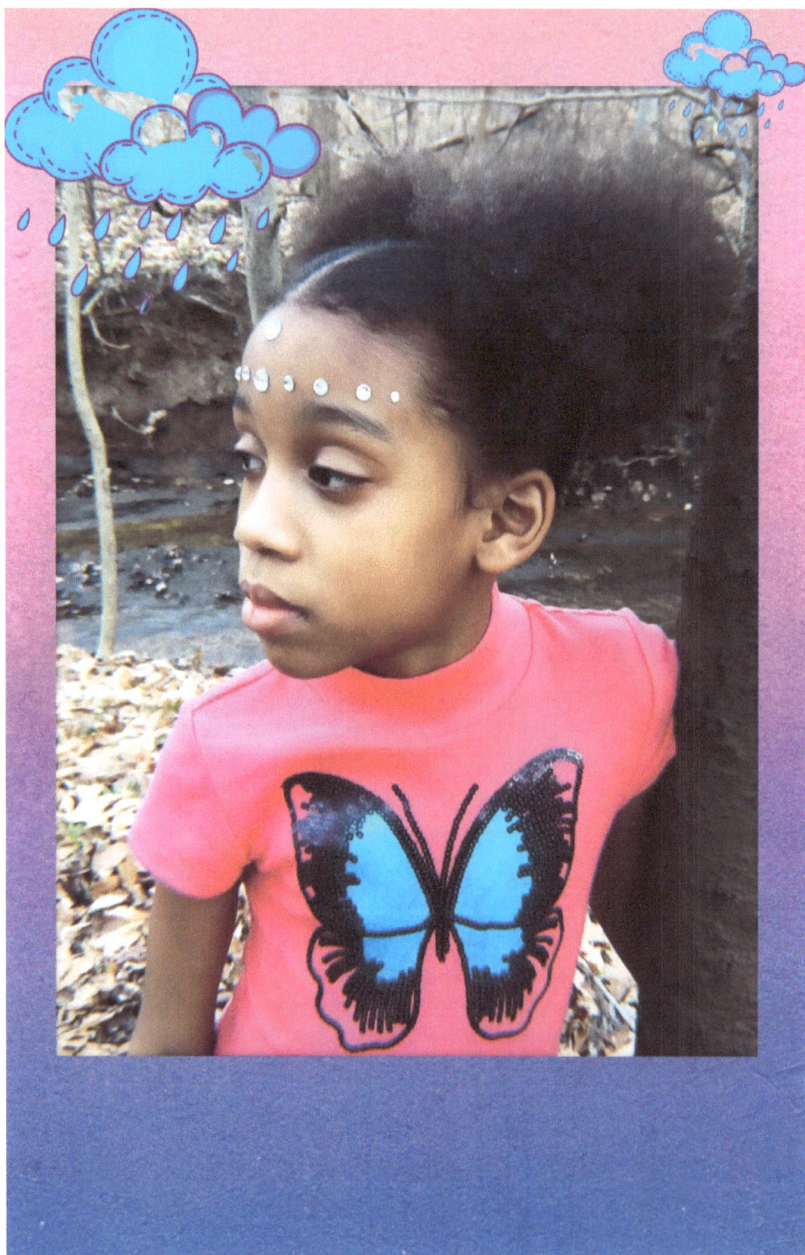

"It makes my hair really short. Shrinkage is the devil Daddy." She stated.

"Shrinkage is the devil? Kiki do you hear yourself?" He questioned.

Kiki didn't care for her father's response too much.

"Come here baby-girl and let me explain something to you." Her father encouraged, as he sat her down on his knee.

"Yes Daddy?" She asked as her eyes lit up with curiosity.

"When I pull your hair straight and it curls back up, would you like to know what that means?" He asked.

"Tell me Daddy." She said.

"It means that your hair is healthy, which means it's still growing, and will continue to grow longer. Always remember Kiki, your hair is your own unique crown that God has blessed you with. No one has a hair-crown quite like you." He assured her.

Kiki flashed her giant Kool-Aid smile.

# KiKi

## Charity

Kiki's Daddy was in the living room cutting up some old clothes. Kiki walked into the living room and sat on the couch beside her father.

"Daddy what are you doing?" She inquired.

"I'm cutting up some old pants into shorts." He replied.

"Daddy can you make me an outfit?" She then requested.

Kiki's father looked at her.

"Kiki, I donated all of you and your brother's old clothes to charity. Kiki when you grow just a little bit more, and then your new clothes become too small, I promise you I will make you an outfit." He explained.

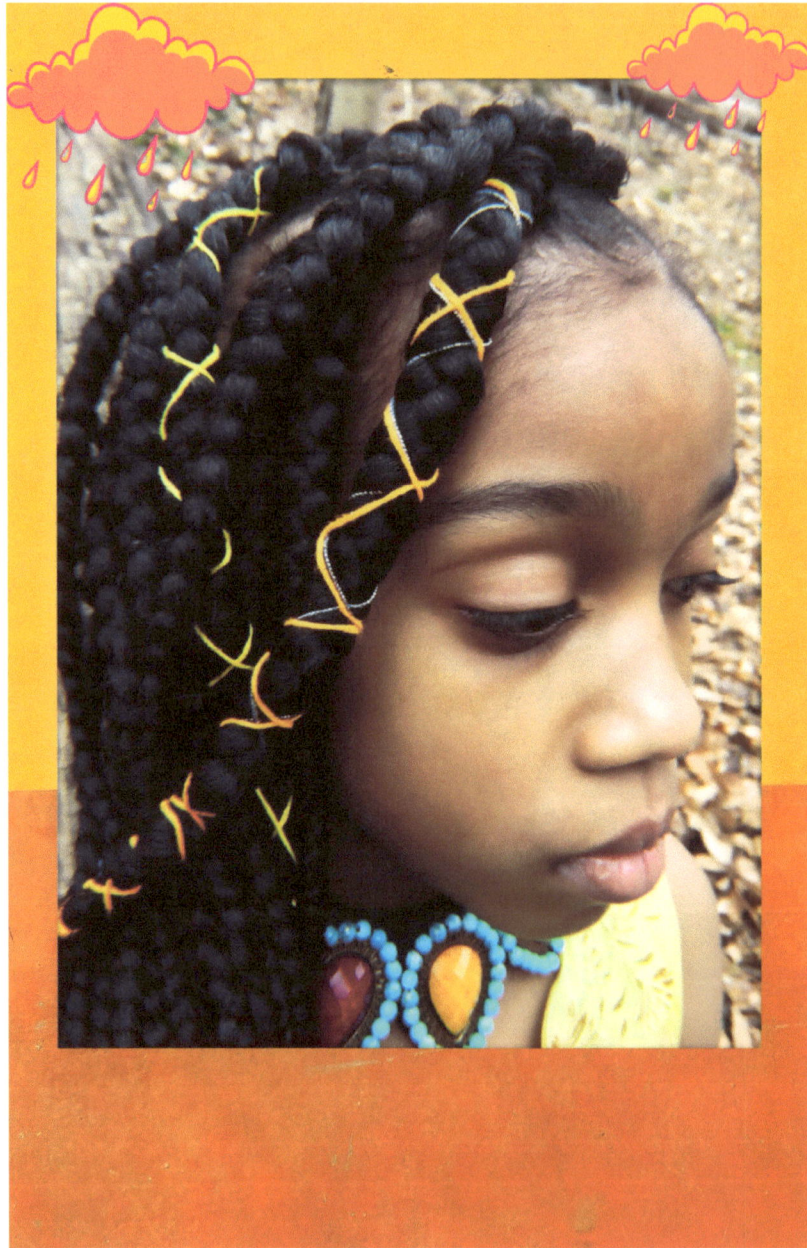

Kiki looked at her father disappointedly. He loathed when his daughter gave him those puppy dog eyes. Her father got up off the couch and went to her closet. He found a summer dress that she hasn't worn in a couple of years. He walked back with the dress to the couch and started cutting away at the dress. Kiki started to smile. Her father put the bottom half of the dress on the floor as she stepped in it. He tied the back of the dress up. Kiki twirled around in the dress.

"You're not done yet Kiki." He said.

Kiki's father placed the top part of the dress around her head. Kiki looked in the mirror and smiled again.

"Ok, Daddy has to do your hair all over again." He said.

Kiki's father was going to do her hair, but he loved the idea of her wearing it out much better. He started to pick out her hair instead. There it was again, Kiki's letdown face.

"What's the matter now?" He asked.

"I don't like my hair Daddy." She said.

"Why?" He asked.

"It's ugly." She replied.

"Kiki your hair isn't ugly when you wear it out naturally. You will understand once you're a little older, I've told you this before. You're beautiful just the way you are and so is your hair." He assured her.

"Ok, all finish Kiki. Now it's time to go outside, so that I can take pictures of the prettiest little girl in the world." He said.

Kiki raced her father to the front door, to take photographs.

# Kiki

# Love Thyself

Kiki's surrounded by girls and women of all ages, with different shades of color, in her everyday life, that has unique hair textures and body shapes. Kiki's father found it to be odd when he noticed Kiki wasn't embracing her natural hair. He hoped and prayed if he wrote a book that

showed her images of herself,
with different hairstyles, Kiki
would come to realize the inner
and outer beauty that she
possessed. Remember mothers
and fathers of the world;
encourage, love, and protect
your children. They're a
reflection of you, and one day,

your children will grow up, to love like you do.

# Be free Kiki, be like a bird and fly...

The End

www.ingramcontent.com/pod-product-compliance
Lightning Source LLC
LaVergne TN
LVHW072132070426
835513LV00002B/77